Breaking Ground

Breaking Ground

Paul Hunter

Paul Hunter

For Linda
— joy in the dirt!

Silverfish Review Press

ACKNOWLEDGMENTS

Section II—"Lay of the Land"—appeared as a Word Works chapbook in a letterpress edition of 300, selected by The Rounce & Coffin Club for their traveling 1998-99 Western Books Exhibition.

Thanks are due to the editors of the following publications:

Tailwind: "Underfoot," "At the Hard Everyday Heart of It," and "Seed"
Pontoon: "Sorry" and "At the Hard Everyday Heart of It"
now it's up to you: "Outhouse" (limited edition broadside)
The Raven Chronicles: "How Deep Down" and "Pioneers"
The Temple: "What It's Come to Hereabouts"
ArtAccess: "Pioneers"

Published by Silverfish Review Press
P.O. Box 3541
Eugene, OR 97403

ISBN: 1-878851-20-9 978-1-878851-20-8

Cover photo Kent Valley © 2002 by Glenn J. Rudolph.
Cover design by Valerie Brewster, Scribe Typography.
Text design by Rodger Moody and Connie Kudura, ProtoType Graphics.

Second Printing 2007
Manufactured in the United States of America.

In memory of
Curwood & Georgianna

Contents

I. Underfoot

Runt

We're not all that big ourselves
the day we make a game of
chasing the runt of the litter
back through the slats of his pen

so tiny formed so perfect black pink white
we itch to hold and finger
the only one who fits through even then
who doesn't know he is caught
who can choose to escape from
the sow on her side like a heaven

letting them all get at her
flowing rivulets where
he would be nudged aside anyhow
so awhile on the illusion
of freedom seems to thrive

as we chase him in out around
the sow who at last shakes herself
while the others under her huddle
makes as if to defend him
rears and snorts

that when we back off
lowers herself with a sigh
resigned to the mounting tide of
a dozen hungry mouths

a game that goes on until Edwin
spots us run the piglet
among us back and forth
and since he can't see it's in fun
has to do something so tells us
running is bad for them
and if we will only leave him be
we can have him
a silly argument that somehow works

so from a distance the next couple weeks
we spy him turn from milk to solid food
slipping out beyond pellets in feed troughs
without any help from the others
by himself to poke around

purple pigweed lush by roadsides
or root up wild carrots
with the pink beginnings of a snout
explore the limp dark of a feed sack
shrieking snorting to get out
or with a shivering dance
catch and crunch down a cricket

till like the autumn of first grade
one day he is too fat
and stopped by the boards simply caught

his tail starts to curl his snout turns
hairy ragged and rough
and soon he is just like the others
all getting ready for market
no curious spirit no magic
and we can't tell them apart

Queenie

If we could catch Queenie ourselves
Uncle Edwin said we could ride

he had an old cavalry saddle
he never used
and the bridle that went with the harness
she wore to work in the garden
had long reins

and after slow dancing
an hour in the pasture
around the rock outcroppings
she would sometimes allow
herself to be cornered
accepting the carrot
to be bridled and saddled and climbed

oftentimes we would give up
when she was not in the mood
and would dodge and run us ragged

just to show three small boys
they are no match for
one sure-footed middle-aged mule

I had already heard about stubborn
how you had to get their attention
with a two by four
then they might do what you wanted
in their own sweet time

and the flopear sex joke of her name
was simply lost on me

but I plain wasn't listening
when he said he'd rather have
her than any horse or tractor
cultivating row crops
because she watched where
she put her feet down
never stepped on
a melon or cuke or anything

didn't much have to be told
when to stop or go either
since she was always right there

so when we did get to ride
all piled up or one at a time
it was not playing cowboy
it was something else entirely
perched atop all that savvy
on the lookout
that could not really be driven

that would never stumble or swerve
no matter how
we sawed the reins to argue
or break into a gallop
no matter how we kicked and yelled

that once aboard just had to let go
since she knew her way around
all these enclosures
and in her own sweet time
would take us out there and back again

To Market

I

With all that fear and nurture
that goes into scratching a living
suddenly arrives the day
market price you milking overhear
from the tinny radio
tucked up under rafters
shit-splattered even there
quarter of five in the a.m.
grain prices beef prices futures

tell yourself settle for this
before it goes any farther
off into greed or depression

knowing how it looms and pounces
how it has caught you before
knowing when you back in to unload
and run down the ramp to a pen
hear the bid and the asking
in a heartbeat known to swerve
and beat you flat like a hailstorm
maybe already too late
no holding back another day
no pulling away pocketing
the feed gas and sleep already spent

still in all you decide to load and haul
your pigs in to market today

and maybe because you have been where
as a boy you had to drive
cattle to market eighty miles
on foot with a long stick to head them
that one way always took you three-four days

your '51 International makes almost a lark
six-ton stake-sided painted red and white

and on a whim
maybe because you're feeling good
or to clear out from underfoot
of beleaguered womenfolk
think to take along the three small boys

wax-paper wrapping meatloaf sandwiches
yours with the big slice of onion
cupcakes cold milk in a thermos

ramp up the pigs at no inconsiderable fuss
set off with them snuffling and restless
to see after a year of corn blight worms and worse
what fate might still have in store

2

At the edge of the fragrant yards
you back up to the dock and run the hogs in
clambering over each other
excited for the moment to be free

walk down the maze of chutes behind them
where men raise the cry pigs a-coming
clamber up side-rails to clear
till you turn into a pen and swing the gate shut

peek in as if for the first time see
how they might look to a stranger
well-fed snouts exploring corners
eternal lookout for a mouthful

then wait perched up on a rail
for buyers in white shirts
with clipboards and curved walking canes
polished from handling livestock

hear the first bid take and hold it
expressionless awhile try to figure
how far from the radio numbers
how likely to rise should you hold out

but this time too good a mood maybe
small boys watch you stick your hand out
saying mister you just bought
yourself some hogs
then ear to ear the grin spread wings

3

And with the money safely folded
inside the bill of sale
buttoned front flap of your overalls
you head back out of town
past the last street light and bus stop
beyond the suburbs slowing to a crawl

at the first mailbox like a bird-house
set out on a fence-post
where starting to breathe free
you flit through lengthening shadows
squint heading west
and stop at last at a crossroads

for late lunch set up on the truckbed
with the boys swinging
caterpillar feet in time together
as they munch a mile high in unison

and the rest of the way home dreamily
drive windows rolled down to smell
clover freshcut and sun-cured
for the bailer chuffing down its windrow
farmer looking up returns a wave

and in the back now three small boys
in among pig droppings
deep in the hay bounce and giggle
digging ice cream out of dixicups
frozen hard flat wooden spoons
licked clean by the turn onto gravel
taste made to last the whole way

At the Hard Everyday Heart of It

Even toward the end perfection:
Edwin's mismatched work team Duke and Bill
Duke a strawberry roan
a towering eighteen hands
with four white feathered hooves
a Shire
Bill a Belgian
shorter wider solid muscle
a dark liver greying at the muzzle
both geldings
a whole life in harness together
only Sundays in deep shade
turned head to tail to switch flies
so linked they raised the same foot to start off

Duke on the left and Bill right
red and black tall and short
no matter what they would pull
plow mower hay wagon
curl up shining iridescent dirt
send the blind blade snickering through the crop

even drowsing standing stamping in their stalls
patient with the harnessing
patient with their bits and blinders
their collars and hames and hitching up
the gruff commandments
giddyup and whoa there gee and haw
the ratcheting click of the tongue
the flat slap of affection on the rump

worked as one
to back out of a tight spot
to take the load lean and pull
or stand rooted while Edwin
knots the reins to the brake
and jumps down to clear away
the tangle from underfoot
then nodding go on pulling straight ahead

Underfoot

Though this country may look ordinary
just small farming in between the hills

things work up out of nowhere each spring thaw
stone axes arrowheads even now and again
Indian skeleton or shooting star

still beyond treasure
underneath these parts run far and wide
a whole other world
of limestone caves they say go forever

and it doesn't happen often but
sometimes away in the corner of a field
or pasture overnight there'll be
a sinkhole open up
that could swallow a church
if any happened by

and when they find it the bravest of the boys
will tie himself to a rope and take a light
and spiral down to the opening
and slip in there while the others
up at the rim hold on
so they can pull and dig
should it let go any minute

and he might be half a day
or pop right back up
blinking and muddy
depending what his light finds
down in all that dark and where it goes
and the strength of his batteries

sometimes the caves are ordinary
but so solid I have heard
a farmer may take and move his house
or build one right over the mouth
so he has all that for cellar storage
or storm shelter
even source of water in a drought

but there too may be crystal palaces
rainbow-painted walls so glorious
pillars reaching down and building up
cathedral domes and bottomless black pools
and every kind of brave boys' lies
the rest of us only dream about

but usually after everyone who dares
has had their look
they dump a load of rock
and tamp the dirt back over it
so no stray animal or child
will fall and get swallowed up
by that other world
we all know is underfoot
deeper than the roots we work
only too dark and too quiet

Sorry

One old farmer who had only daughters
that when they started to ripen considered
none of us local boys ever quite good enough

for a while there laboring to decide
which city college to send them as
none of the three ever much favored opening books

began to have kind of a mailbox problem
which pritnear every night then would explode
from a cherry bomb or ball bat

or hit off the bumper of a speeding car
sail in the ditch or the cornfield
where he would find it next morning

straighten out best as he could and prop back
which as you know can get old
and even when it turned up missing

wasn't no way stopping Lonnie
who loved any excuse to hand-deliver
college mail to sweet young things himself

and the deputy sheriff in these parts
when the call came in from Ed Holtz
destruction of property et cetera

said he would run on out have a look
when he had a minute but figured
some kind of courting ritual he should

leave well enough alone to run its course
seeing as peacekeeping his bounden duty
never said boo about making no federal case

so Ed finally reckoned it was all up to himself
and after spending chilly nights out in a sleeping bag
being woken up time and again by the old slam bang

fired up the forge from when he had horses and welded
a plate of steel on the end of half a railroad rail
and pounded the thing twelve feet down in the ground

and bolted the old mailbox back on top
doing the whole thing late one night after dark
not telling the girls or his wife one whisper about it

and waited out in the field there and fell asleep
and woke to a godalmighty crash
jumped up and there we all set

an old jalopy hung up on his trap
two heads through the windshield
four of us boys all pretty shaken up

and everyone so sorry sorry
none more so than Edward Holtz himself
as he picked up and held every one of us

as if we were his own
tearful and thankful and amazed
at what his life had run up against

Worn Bright

Everything is old and backward
broken twice mended worn bright
and I am the bigcity kid
getting his hands black acquiring
the so-called country facts of life

when we go into town for the first time
to fill up Bill's DeSoto turtleback
with coal and drive on the scale
a second time for the weigh-out
I watch the big guy bump along
the weights with a stump for a thumb
squint and call out the numbers
watch Bill pay from
a black leather purse that snaps shut
keeps in the bib of his overalls
with the pencil stub and specs

then I go into the hardware
and buy me a harness strap
for a belt and have to cut
a whole yard off the tail end
and out in the middle of nowhere
punch me one hole for starters
so my new pants will stay up

then we stop for lunch
in a dark little diner
with flypaper coils off the ceiling
with a screen door at the front and one in back
that when the front one yawns
screeches on its spring and claps
a second later the back one snaps

which it does when another skinny little Bill
who drives the feed truck
that I never see smile much less talk
saunters in and sits with us
orders a steak and potatoes

Bill says how do you mean to eat that
Bill says you watch and learn something
like the pair of screen doors back to back

and when it comes
halfway through our bean soup
biscuits and gravy
he whips out a big pocket knife
dices the whole thing to tatters
like he's fixing to feed a small child
slathers catchup all over
and proceeds to shovel down
while we try not to look

and when it's all gone
he reaches in his shirt pocket
I think for his teeth at long last
but it's the makings he rolls up like
scratching behind one ear
pulls out of nowhere
licks it shut flicks a match
on his thumbnail and lights

says I may not have much of a bite left
but I can still gum it to death

Start the Day

Rolled not cut he would say
to me kneedeep in gold
with the one big aluminum shovel
at the grain elevator
six tons in the wagon weighed
to be shoveled down a wood chute
and turned into cash money

rolled not cut oats
me without breakfast
a big wad of kernels
tucked in the one cheek
to soften and chew on
combined fresh
from the field before sundown
here fresh from bed
in my same dirt-stiff clothes
jostled the six miles to town
on gravel back roads
at ten miles an hour
tractor straining the full load

that when you take it
feel tongue and hitch stretch
feel whatever play and give

rolled not cut and
no such thing as quick oats
arguing how long it takes
on a wood stove to boil water
even with split kindling handy

and all the different ways
you can serve up your oats
boil up right now or
soak overnight and
fry up in a skillet

every way fine and dandy
creamy or crunchy
anywhere in between
long as you got milk
and brown sugar
to go on top
maybe a handful of raisins
long as it isn't quick oats
chopped up with steel knives
in a factory
not run between rollers the old way
made bitter I swear
I can taste a real difference
and quick is no way to start the day

Cowboy

Up to the moment the semi lowers its ramp
and out in the yard stumble forty-one
scrawny feeder calves blinking and bawling

like any boy all I want is to be
riding off into mountains under the vast
purple sky of my dreams a true cowboy

but here are only mole-hills
all fenced in ordinary
but for runoff gullies and gulches flat as a tabletop
and every horse I work around has meant business
even swayback sleepwalkers turn skitterish
like to kick your teeth loose
nothing between the ears but a quivering knot
still a raw nerve in there somewhere might
take a notion any blowing leaf's a snake rared up to strike
spark the dynamite
take the bit buck and bolt

so there's no horse on hand here to round up
these calves fresh from Texas
that on the way north inspected
got tagged for a raging pinkeye epidemic
that has to be treated pronto

and Bill is smart and strong but old and a little slow
so I am elected to rope every one
on foot with a coil of stiff new three-quarter-inch hemp
snub it up to a fencepost
bulldog it to the ground hold its head down
while he squirts stinging pink goop into each rolling eye

then let it up herd it off to a pen
cut out rope run down wrestle and capture
another and do it all over

and though by late in the day the lasso drops quicker
without so much of a twirl
I get dragged and thrown around plenty

and naturally the biggest saves himself for last
a rangy black yearling bullcalf that'll go
a good four hundred pounds
stone blind in one eye with a mean pair of horns
sharp pointed straight ahead

so after the first big run-around a couple near misses
that dip and hook my worst nightmares
we take a breather let him settle down
try to figure a way

and what we do is each take a loose gate in two hands
to box him in a corner
but the gate's too heavy he spins out in-between
then we string a long rope cut the barnyard in half
and while we close in one end he hooks a horn under
yanks me a handful of splinters

and though I know there is no such thing
by this time I'm down to even wishing a smart horse
like rodeos I have seen would come prancing
along this gravel road sidewise full of sass
and skitter up to intimidate and outsmart this bullcalf

so I say so out loud
and Bill and I look at each other
through the long shadows
and see there is no other way
and next thing we know Bill has the lariat
behind his back in the yard hid where he leans
up next to the stoutest old snubbing-post
and I'm charging the calf in there feinting and bluffing
this way and that like a cow pony
circling around toward his blind side
waving and shouting to herd him
always coming at him
ignoring the horns watch the front feet
back and forth hup back and forth

till he moves about just where we want him
weaves and staggers and balks
then in slow motion Bill settles
the loop on his horns and we close in
heave together once and drop

Making Hay

Full summer wade in the field
every bloom awake alive with bees
pull and taste a sweet sprig of
alfalfa red clover timothy
tip your cap back eye the day

weathercock to the wind
to sniff out moisture
as once begun you will need
a couple-three long hot dry ones
every strong back and hard hand
to make all your hay and put by

so give the word mow early and let lay
then rake in windrows
and under the hot hand of noon
pass through the fields to turn again
worry each wisp in the sky
could bring ruin stand and watch
leaves wilt to green nutrient
smell and feel fresh scarcely dry

then at a nod fire the tractor
and start the third time down the row
feel bailer push out the first
like a birth stop to heft
decide if the crop is really
too late too soon about perfect

then begin the long haul
circling the field
every bale lifted and thrown
boosted by knee shoulder elbow
further the final ones flung
to the man on top stacking
onto the wagon drawn to
the far end of the field
mounting a teetering summit

then the slow run for the barn
where aloft begin building
a giant staircase as you climb
the sun-warm green-gold mountain
toward evening blue
silver tin roof shot with stars
pile another aching fragrant heaven
pitchdark kingdom come now rafter high

Spry

You couldn't call him slow
at his age sixty-four just deliberate
with plenty of what they call spry
that unspent youth poised
in the mow on the edge of a rafter
still not quite flown away

not that he would jump up in the air
click his heels at a barn dance mind you
what anyone middle-aged might start to see
as a pure waste of energy

but he could do anything I could
at fifteen sunup to sundown

and when I fell off that hay wagon
pitched forward underneath the wheels
had both legs run over just like that
and blacked out though they say
I gave one long howl like a banshee
he snatched the hand clutch hit the brakes
on the John Deere right then to stop her
before the back wheels could finish me

Because For Once There Was Too Much

In the little unpainted house neatly made of two rooms
with no more windows now no more stove
no cupboards not a stick of furniture
with only the tight roof left to hold storms out
and the one shut door

we took empty tin cans opened flat to nail over
mouse holes and rat holes
in the floor the baseboards all around the walls

then where porch and steps had long since slumped away
pulled the wagon up to the doorway practically level
though you could see under where the house stood
up on great blocks of crick rock
under where the skunk made her den and raised pups
so others kept their distance

and shoveled it full to the windows
hissing sweating shoveled half a day
threatening to rain all the while
shoveled it full to where if there had been a table
in the front room to sit at any more
your pockets would have been full
riches lapping your belt buckle

or if there had been a bed in the back room
and you lay down
there would have been all that hard gold
in your toes in your hair

as there was when I took my shoes off
to pour out and lay down a minute
to wait for wheat prices to rise
or the rain to blow sideways and ruin it

Outhouse

Not always such a nuisance
to just get up and go
some nights fresh out of the warm nest
like this one asleep in the attic
no thought to using the thundermug
tucked at the foot of the bed
that some nights might wake others
but even here alone
is not quite right to rid yourself
of something eaten somewhere don't set right

so slip out of bed into
your hightop work shoes
feel the sweat of the day cooled
to a rattling fit without socks
leave the laces trailing and shuffle
through dark house down
wood then stone steps to the yard
through grass wet with dew
scuffling your feet in fair warning
for the damp toad planted in the path
or the rippling weeds of
the stalking blacksnake or barn cat
or in this moonlight long-nosed hollow-eyed
opossum like a bone-white ghost
darting from underfoot
or just the skunk's telltale stripe
wobbling in tall grass
meandering blindly for crickets
that don't know enough to shut up

and always these warm nights
through my dreaming stumble
lightning bugs that flare up on the rise
tree frogs whippoorwills
reduplicating themselves
and always the cicadas and the owls

till I reach the outhouse
with its moon-sign door sprung wide
to light the business
grope my way into the shadows
turn back the hinged lid
settle onto the worn wooden seat
over the fragrant airy void
look up through locust branches to the stars
sit there dozing dreaming long and long
as meteors flare and burn
breathing in the full night all around
feeling my guts at last ease
away into nothingness
out of the great dark and back again

hearing nothing
but the scrape of my own shoes
as I heave up and
with my pants at my ankles
gently rap twice on
the lid of the upside-down coffee can
so if there is a mouse like last night
chewing herself a nest
of the whole roll of toilet paper
she will know to escape
and not tumble out in my hand
both of us dreaming
so deep we stare wide-eyed forever
akin and intimate
neither one inclined to run away

II. Lay of the Land

Reckoning

—homage to William Ward

1

Having raised them every one handfed
and dug some out of snow and carried in
or towed up out of wallows in the crick
and nursed the sick ones
pinkeye lungworm scabies scours
you name it back to health
nobody blamed him loading up the truck
for market letting go the care
longfaced and slow come time for it

but what was hard
he'd wave his arms and shout
around the ring just like the rest
and swing his stick
and make as if to hit it on the snout
but then the damn fool thing would run
through him like nothing
pick him out and shame him like
he was a broken gate
like he was the barn door left open
the schoolteacher come sunny judgment day
who just so happened stood
between them and their one taste
of whatever the hell it was all about

2

He had a bullcalf one time sick so bad
it lay there in the straw and fouled itself
all through one winter
while he spooned it milk and warm mush
and held it to keep it quiet

till the bright blades of spring
finally sliced clear back into the stall
and he helped it to its feet
and watched it sink because
its front legs had stiffened
couldn't straighten up

and he called the vet out to look
but the man shook his head
and nicked the calf's tendons
with a sharp knife
and said you have to make it stand
to stretch those legs out
or it's finished

so several times a day
he would chase it around
the barn and flail his arms
shouting go on get out of here
but it had to be ground for hamburger
because not once did it ever
take a step up off its knees

3

The little fingers of both hands
would not lie straight
from being wrapped around
a hickory handle sixty-some-odd years
and even pushed down on a table
wouldn't flatten

he had other flaws:

he couldn't wait to drink his coffee
and slopping it into the saucer
set the cup aside to slurp and blow

and he kept the pricetag
on the lens of his dimestore spectacles
and forced himself to look around it
so no one would think
he really much needed glasses

and worse yet he could not abide a scab
and would pick at wherever he'd hurt himself
day after day till it ran red
and in time the little scratch became a scar
that healed in spite of him

4

His favorite pastime
at the county fairs
was watching tractor pulls because
no one got hurt
no matter how you kicked or cussed
the tractors wouldn't snort or roll their eyes
at worst a thing would break down
smoke and clatter to get fixed
and it was a true test
someone always won or lost

besides which some old boys
would oftentimes hitch up
to the sledge of concrete blocks
their rusty everyday machines
splattered with mud fresh from plowing
and go up against the dealers
in their whitewalls and waxjobs
and loud clip-on bowties
perched on high in air-conditioned cabs
and know just enough about snatching
a load and getting moving
sometimes to feather the clutch out
and walk away with a prize

5

He'd say you could tell a real farmer
just take a look at his tools
and point to the plow of a neighbor
stuck in the end of its furrow
awaiting spring to turn around

Even letting the ax
stick in the wet chopping block
for him was a little much
though with no room in the barn
his own handcrank '32 John Deere
stood out its seat roofed with plywood
and a lard can on the stack that
blew forty feet when
it would cough and try starting

6

If it was his he would sooner
kick out the fence posts he'd jammed
up under the eaves of the woodshed
leaning swaybacked from that windstorm
he'd tried to pull straight with the tractor

but tenant farmer it's never
his to build up or let fall
just duck in for an armload
of wood twice a day and
pray to slip out from under

7

One winter morning clearing out
a cabin on one corner of the place
pieced together in the Depression
a crazy quilt of foreclosures

he built up a blaze in the fireplace
and got in too much of a hurry
said he kind of hypnotized himself
just a quick look and toss
broken toys moldy books
any useless godforsaken thing
left in a rush to have done with
this deadend till he came to
a can of blasting powder
looked at what it was
tossed it right in the fire
before he could stop himself
and was standing there staring
when it blew
bricks out the back into the yard
flaming rubbish all across the room
singed off his hair and eyebrows
around the union cap he says
a good thing he keeps screwed on tight

8

Plowing harrowing drilling
cultivating picking he would say
so many times you go
up and down these rows
gets tough to follow
each wiggle over and over

but you start straight
and mind your business
goes along pretty easy

though all the same he would veer
wide at the sight of
a nesting pair of killdeer
or wind around a hillside
and make work for himself
to follow the lay of the land
and catch the runoff

9

And too there was
how his striped wallpaper ran
straight up one wall over molding
across the ceiling down the other side
so sitting in their livingroom felt like
being wrapped inside
an oldtime Christmas present

and on one wall two framed pictures:
mournful Jesus looking down
offering his thorny flaming heart
to an Indian on a pony
praying in the sunset on a mountain
eyeless head back arms wide

10

Everything has its moment
he says taken at the height
even field corn whose huge ears
bear kernels the size of a banty egg
even horse corn that stands
seven-eight feet at the shoulder
tassling out golden overhead
hard as flint in the corncrib
so hard the cattle's teeth grind down
and even barn rats go at it
loud enough to wake the living dead

even the toughest hybrid dent
watched over from the first
shucking a few on the stalk
testing by smell and by color
grooving each face with a thumbnail
till late one sultry day
he declares it ripe

and backs his '47 DeSoto
up to the end of a row
we tear along and pile the trunk full
and drive home straight to the pot
of boiling salted water

it can't help but be tender
and so sweet his skinny old frame
will polish off a couple dozen
ears this one sitting
with a heel of bread to twirl in butter
and a bucket to catch the dead soldiers
as one after the other
with a clang they're tossed aside

II

Though no one is perfect
in bib overalls and frayed work shirt
rolled twice each wrist for
the freedom he came close

good looking at sixty-four
hardworking lean and tough
unfailingly polite
he never spoke
two words where one would do
or one if he could nod and point

he had got out of the habit
of speaking his mind
in a land where it didn't matter
where everyone planted
the same pretty much
harvested what came up

besides which he had no children
with an ailing taciturn wife
who enjoyed TV and fishing

but once I got him started
at fifteen over posthole digging
stretching wire
stacking hay bales
pitching out manure
he got into the swing of it
and like spring cleaning
tossed out practically everything
back in there saved up

thoughts like mushrooms
raised in caves
like blind white newts
that blinked and fought
the hold of your hip pocket
like peach halves put up right

how particular he was
buckling his knickers as a boy
and from the turn of the century
the first joke that tickled
of a pretty girl in an outhouse
and two rubes in the bushes to watch

and when someone tore through
the old cemetery where
they'd go to scare themselves
and knocked over all the headstones
how they shook in holy terror

and working for others what he had
wasn't much to show for
all that honest quiet of a life
but soft and hard he knew what he knew
and when you planted
right what became of it
and when I think of a good man
he is mostly what still comes to mind
after all the rest
have been loaded and driven to market

How Deep Down

Before sunup in the damp air
there is room to swing the pick
break through the nest of roots
and hardpan like a slab

We work fast to punch in
and be out of the sun
before it's well up
two dry old men in overalls
and a boy sweating like one

By the time we get to heavier
going there is no room
so in turn we work
shovel prybar posthole digger
and take it a bite at a time
making a neat round hole
trying to keep it straight
because who knows how deep
down it'll want to get

Red then yellow clay then blue
straight down through fossil rock
straight into the mother
breathing hard so don't rush it
one man down at a time
the ladder lowered and pulled out
dampening now as it sinks like
an outhouse in the swamp

One digs away while the others
lean on their elbows
and talk over the mouth
endless old witching stories
willow apple or peach forks
or ells of thick copper wire
like the pair passed over this field
that wobbled hunted then crossed
on this exact spot

Reminiscing a kind of low music
of cats swimming then rabbits
tree climbing then old jokes
talk that steers clear of dry holes
careful not to kick dirt on
the digger helpless beneath them
who grunts at his handle and listens

Thunderheads in a cloud patch pass
so bright it hurts to look up
still in that airless dark
with all these leathery whispers
like swallows scissoring
the biting insects of doubt

Now and then he sings out for
the canvas bucket lowered on a rope
to clear out underfoot
or calls for the water jug   .
on a line through its finger loop

or the ladder when he just can't stand
the slippery narrow feel and dank
of being buried alive a minute longer
and lets one of the yarnspinners
take a turn for old time's sake

Around noon when the sun stabs
twenty feet in we knock off
sprawl under a tree for sandwiches
splash a little water on each other
and smear our clown makeup

But as soon as there is shade
again one eases in
to dig for the last of it

And by sundown hear underfoot
that sucking sound
that sends one after a lantern
to lower for a look
at how strong it's coming in
or how much more to dig for it

and planted at last like a tripod
around the hot tired mouth
still in the afterglow
of a tin cup we draw out
a muddy fistful of its cool wet light
smack our lips
and pronounce it sweet

Manure

That summer spread a hundred tons myself
on top of the hundred with him digging alongside
through all five barns around the patchwork place
built up underfoot to where
the cows hit their heads on the rafters
and he said it was that or raise rabbits
or saw off their damn legs
so we chipped away every spare minute

perfect job for a greenhorn
chewing apart levering muscling up
this pungent cake part bedding-straw part feed
some bog some ferment some dry rot
some with mushrooms poking out
fragrant a foot down as a rare old cheese
aged to a solid ripe fundament

new earth surprising every bite
with the squirming pink fingers
of a handful of baby rats
a green horse collar or swingletree
a sleepy blacksnake full of lumps
coal scuttle harness buckle
blue patent medicine bottle
stash of a secret drinker in the muck

all to be loaded and broadcast
on stubble fields and turned under
with no way of doing it not right

so at first I took a silage fork
and went in for a bigger bite
maybe pumped to get it over in a day
but slowed when I saw how little
a dent we made by sundown
and next day went back to the pitchfork

and Bill would lean admire my swing
and call me a natural
said I might get to be
kind of a what you call connoisseur
get so I could tell all the different
flavors and what they've been eating

and took me around to sample
one corner where some years before
hogs had been penned
another where some ewes had wintered
once and lambed
stalls where they'd kept a span of mules
or horses he couldn't be positive
and naturally the chickens everywhere
they could roost or scratch or brood

why you'll get so you even miss the smell
and can't get to sleep nights
without a fresh pile for a pillow

and he was right pretty quick I got to know
the thin flaccid pancakes of cattle
the sheep's ripe plums
the pigs' gold smear and dribble
chickens' salt and pepper candle drippings
the geese great cake decorations
and horse blueblack chunks of evil

so we would back the spreader in
this long narrow hearse on iron wheels
that had once been horsedrawn
that had a chaindriven feeder
and three wicked whirling sets of blades

and when we had it mounded up
to where it couldn't take another bite
he'd let me fire up the tractor
and go tearing off down the field
racing the wind flies aroma
in top gear at a dozen miles an hour
spewing a brown blizzard far and wide
that left me emptied out skyhigh and satisfied

What It's Come To Hereabouts

1

You could say it all builds up
the big and little things
how hungry-eyed the young ones watch TV
till they can't help but want what you can't buy

and how the things they peddle
you don't half see the need
reach out at you from the city
and some way slip under the door
where at least you could once keep
that dog-eared Sears catalogue
put up half the year in a drawer

then there's just how people sprawl
paving the back country roads
running the water and power
out to their split level heavens
driving land prices up to where
the only thing left is to roll out
the hot asphalt and throw up
condos and factory outlets
over good prime bottom land
yourself and beat them to market

2

Though with us it all started
back around the radio
even then the old man would mutter
now don't you go getting ideas

but really it begins just getting by
when you take the job as night watchman
at the distillery in town because you're young
and can practically sleep leaning on your hoe
or pick up a little diesel and tire work
at the truckstop out by the Interstate
to tide you over

because the size of things never fazed you
once you've worked a breeder bull
on a short lead up close to his business
that he wants to get after
so bad he'll clear a six foot fence
with you hanging onto
that slobbery ring out of ignorance

and you always could fix anything
or rig it to work in the meantime
a little wire and a bent nail
till you get your mowing done
your hay put by
your oats and wheat in the barn
your pears put up
then fix it right
because that's all a farmer is
mister handyman

3

So before you know it you're in the dark
and tunneling both ways
counting on the paycheck
hearing the roof drip
as things fall down around your ears
there's no time or daylight to patch up

4

And settle in the rut of steady money
driving school bus and snowplow
and summer three months solid
work on the country roadcrew
making your own hay past midnight
staggering in broad daylight to hook up
the shiny milking machines
no way you could pay for today

and always the long drive unwinding
back roads to and from the job
not like the walk in from the field
where you might shut down
the tractor smoking hot where it stands
up to its axle in furrows
that gleam with lost light
ground curled in stiff waves
broke open for the seed
last year's dead roots
weed and crop alike
dearth and upheaval and promise
still knit together up ahead

where the bell and call to supper waver
in a distance all its own
that makes you strike out in a beeline
leaving fresh tracks as you stumble
across the soft uneven ground

5

And though somehow you hang in there
it all seems to come down to
the few things a year you can decide:
sell off the hay or feed it
plant more oats this year
or stay in corn
breed the shoats or
take a chance on feeder calves
that when you unload
still seem full of wonder
at what on earth has possessed them
and hold you awhile in vacant stares

but where does it wind up in the end
but selling off
granddad's nickel-studded double harness
green with mold to antique hounds
decades after the last of the Belgians
its great pulling heart put to pasture
toppled and sagged and was turned under

so first it's coal oil lamps and rocker
then the churn and clock and chiffarobe

until where it ends is an oasis
a cluster of old buildings kept up nice
an entry framed in sunken wagon wheels
with a satellite dish
and the land all around it subdivided
with a riding lawnmower
and a vegetable garden reminder
and maybe a few whiteface
calves like ghosts in the half light
still milling around and lowing to be fed

Threshold

Out of the patchwork quilt
of all that used to be
good times and hard
a hundred years and more
surely they salvaged a little
flooring windows doors
places to stand
empty mouths eyeholes

but what won't move
or be torn up like
pegged poplar timbers
sillplates trued by eye
must be heaped and burned

and worse:
ma and pa shade maples cut
their stumps rooted and blasted
the well choked with
chunks of fieldstone foundation
the rusted cookstove
dumped in the outhouse hole
the yard harrowed and planted

Yet with all sign carted off
leveled scattered
snarled fenceline unstrung
rutted road plowed under
old lives overgrown
still every spring
up through winter wheat
clover alfalfa far as you can see
steal iris and crocus and tiger lily
to set a spell at these doorsteps

III. Put By

Standing True

Along fencerows gullies windbreaks
down crickbeds wandering off
scrub pasture wouldn't keep a goat
these beings extend and remember
the freshly lit tips of their lives

outward to one another
in season stretched interlacing
their pale green underthings
that screen all other transactions
in their steady intercourse

oftentimes lopped off at head and foot
hammered in badlands clay and rock
Tennessee red cedar mockorange locust
fenceposts sprout even swallow
bobwire in a mildmannered afterlife

they must sense they are the route
the rest and shelter
the boulevard of so many
who flit along with the seasons
slip among crops and steal off

only in woodlots permitted
the primeval game of shooting up
to patch the torn green tenting overhead
and rooted centuries what more
need any know of life than standing true

even one left alone in a field
in despair of touching kindred
all around plowed and planted
or noon shade for the herd
and last of its kind is no outpost

it takes as its shape the whole sky
and spread wide muscled deep
makes of its canopy a heaven
that in time will draw home
to it every living thing for miles

Invitation

Look how one plum stands an invitation
full of the jabber of small birds
waving all its open arms

wherever it was spit out or thrown it took root
fed by the seed pod a moment
then unfolding out of that young self
stood without complaint
at once in competition
with siblings parents a riot
that swaying sensed earth and sky coursing through it

just under the rough bark most alive
a reach a hydraulic trick of the water
to all but take flight

still as good as practically anything
short of skipping and singing
we can think of to do with a life
and look at us
do we stand beckoning
do we dance about skipping and singing

Sweet Being

The deer will eat
an apple tree clean to the ground
in its leafy infancy
and should it reach again
for a while strip its skin
grind to nothing its twigs
as a delicacy

but amid confused abundance
should one grow
out of reach overlooked
its trunk gets unpalatable
rough
the sweet being
once all one
no longer evident
under scarred heavy bark
the sweet being
sensed now as longing overhead
as flower and fruit

Pioneers

Wherever they move they leave tracks
break trails roll out roads

Where they stop a few hours
they make shelter start fire
kill to feed their hunger

where they stay awhile
they cut down trees
dam water dig holes
put up walls close doors
scatter their seed and wonder

burning up the night
soon they cut down the dark
and set it against itself
they cage animals keep pets
mark down what is theirs
as well as what is not

escaping in time
these rough enclosures
their young soon scale
whatever is on high
swing out and splash
their paint like blood
enter caves and feel
their way clear to the bottom

eventually they plant flowers
to hide their shame raise up trees
cut holes in walls to look away
hang mirrors
bury the dead that lie around
discourage newcomers
by erecting signs
that point everywhere at once
obscuring the devious
ways they come and go

Seed

Where they fall the earth may not be
moist and rich from long labor
crumbled fine to receive them
much less tamped home turned under

where they fall may be stone barren
sand or salt flat with every
fissure or toehold long taken

or where they fall may simply be
among other more vigorous lives
that with a headstart push edgewise
to shoulder outreach overshadow
every new life around
so those underfoot will forever
remain small enough to eat crumbs

yet blown dry lost withered suspended
scattered in deserts millennia
or at the fresh heart of the fruit
and nourishing as manna

it is after all the seed's business
to find its way to earth and bruised
from the fall take its chances
and however it may work its way
let the warm moist dark inside
answer and swell and begin

Crop

Near full grown you wade into
the picture of bounty of promise
its waves on the wind like a sea
all one green thing and nothing
but that one thing turning gold
sprung from the bare open earth
tended expected never once ignored

with here and there an intruder
pigweed burdock wild onion
reminders what it is like
to take hold and stay on
an outsider all your life

in the field in the stalk the long wait
each taste of the hard green seed
a frightening pleasure
careful not to want too much
what can come to nothing
parched or drowned
eaten alive or beaten flat
taken today now this minute
even out of the strong hand
reaching toward the mouth

Threshing

Dawn the day each knows his place
wade into the field
heavy bearded rustling
snap the head clean off one stalk
rub between palms
fingers split a basket blowing chaff
lift one or two taste and see

what the wait and care have been about
the dense hard oval grain
with its hearty dry smell
its longways groove down the middle
where on a moistened swollen kernel
the finger of life would begin
the split of living

and at a nod first
the horsedrawn mower snickers through
the nodding golden grain
then raked and tied in shocks
stacked and loaded just so
for the wagon for the ride

then the tarp is rolled back
the rust-splotched elderly machine
drawn from the dark under cover
to the barnyard the accustomed level place
its steel-lugged wheels chocked
oilcan lifted flywheel given a spin
to remind it of its many motions
how it rustles whirs and clicks
and all the while on its axles rocks

and with oil and grease to the fittings
each bearing every moving part
then the drive belt slung to the tractor
blocked twenty feet off
and pampered adjusted set running

with this job bigger than any one
to get the crop in the right moment
together bought this machine
a tool that will take every one of them
to service feed and run
to haul quickly farm to farm
through this hot dry harvest time

now with each man to his task
where it stands to be fed the first shock
of wheat barley oats gathered up
on this place to the last

maw fed wide from above
metal spout spews straw and chaff
onto a twenty foot stack
where it stays until forked underfoot
or spread on the fields and used up
where by late winter there will be
golden hollows to hide in
green sprouts overarching rain-soaked thatch

but now close to the rumbling whirring guts
men offer the low mouth their sacks
until they're spilled full and tied off
lugged aside stacked

and the women up before dawn bake
and stir chop and set creaking tables
sawhorses and planks on the lawn
lined along under shade trees
for the noon meal
where they will eat everything
doze in the shade twenty minutes
then go straight back to work

till good and done time to move on
to the next farm come morning
saying amen to this one
with not a husk
not a flicker of light left

On The Old Place

You might think Fall is the payoff
when you come to the year's reckoning
and make the most of the crops:
what is grown gathered sold against
what is eaten owed broken and lost

and there does come that moment
sometimes of happy exhaustion
when you feel giddy and wild
to know in your muscles
all you have safely put by

even bad years strain and futility
like a dry season-long funeral
or harvest thunderclap—
ache that has gone in the ground
hope that is now simply done

but the sweetest time on the old place
may be the overdue rest
under comforter and quilt
while the storm rattles windows
the livestock stand pungent and close
and the firewood for the winter
stacked under shelter like gold
in the stove begins thumping its heartbeat
singing to give up its ghost

Retirement

Gets so you learn to love
the gathering dark
the expectant lateness the quiet
standing kneedeep in it barefoot
like a fencepost unstrung
cut free of rusty traces
that formerly sang clawed and stung

now wandering with others
behind and out ahead
across abandoned pasture
with no thought to separate
hold out or in
any other living being

you feel a sort of tune
and the slowest of dances
weave down the line through you
feel your soft footing
go as you lean over
studying puddles for
what there is left of yourself

Harness

After the team was retired
the harness hung by the entryway
drooping on its pegs that last
shambling stumbling couple years
swayback sagging belly
the only things hitching one day to the next
a pat snort of oats withered apple

and when one then the other
right after went into the ground
the harness still hung there awhile
beyond letting go
cobwebbed sweat-stiffened untouched
rivets turned green eyes surrounding
old shapes faint whispers of mold

that once a winter for decades
had been lifted to wipe mend and oil

given attention and care for
all it must hold together
make a team and more
make of Edwin Duke Bill the work one
planted in dirt underfoot
pulling plow rake wagon mower

and though these implements
that could be hitched to a tractor
still linger on the old harness
if it hasn't been let go too long
demands to be cleaned up and flexed
until ready to take on and hold
the working shapes of a team
and once more handed down
to settle and buckle around us

Belongings

As if to remind us
of the body's dispersal
back to its elements
till after a short time
only the hardest handful
remains the one place one ended

so the things that a body
gathers first out of need
then keeps hoarding
tools in vestigial pockets
linger on time out of mind
till past the end
any object treated as friendly
must long to be forgotten

so out of the mainstream one gathers
a few pictures images books
bits of wood cunningly fashioned
stones metals papers
coverings instruments
cloth paint feather skin bone
scraps of nevermind whatnot

that in that instant are signaled
to return to the living
via bequest and memento
via deception and outright theft
flame and sword even
salvation army goodwill and trashheap

passing on the sweet shine of use
the gleam of the substantial
among the lacy tattering
release of the insubstantial
to begin again the migration
of things beyond rightful owners
caught up carried on let go
like so many stones in the road
winding down alongside rushing waters

Straight To Work

Dulled by rust and abuse
blunted bent useless
mislaid underfoot kicked aside
now finally bereft
who does not drop to his knees
fingers spread wide feel around
among weeds and rubbish
wanting for his tools
all he should want for himself

a hook a drawer a shelf
a little home
alongside the others
where one can always be found
where you return
from each lending each borrowing
each hard use
each mending and sharpening
where wiped clean lightly oiled
you will be found
lifted and turned to the light
sweetly fitting the hand
as you were meant to
and sit poised to begin

For The Miracle

In the shop its bench work-scarred
long planks run under the window
where grease meets paint meets sawtooth chisel
where an engine would be heaved to take apart
and at one end vise jaws parted
having said the final word let go

and in the center of the gloom
underneath a caged lightbulb
the anvil spiked to a tree stump
where things may be heated and lifted
beaten down turned into one
and in place of a potbellied stove
the forge festooned with blackened tools

and on shelves underfoot rows of coffee cans
to sort by size wingnut from locknut
from wood screw machine screw
bent nail fence steeple hose clamp

and beyond all around broken things
brought here for the miracle
alongside things in their rude beginnings
that may yet be finished and praised
amid things in the way once too often
that may become raw materials
and out of their great beyond serve in turn as
patch or knife blade or chair rung
to be of use once again

Outskirts

I

So many alive now began
with a barn out back but no land
or wire fence behind the tract home
abutted against endless acres
of sorghum buckwheat cotton
cantaloupe groping beneath
the pirouettes of screeling irrigation
or grazing headdown
persistent sheep switching cattle
with their mild curiosities
even skittish horses
willing to be talked to handfed
by any child a few moments
to discover what an offering
poked through this fence might taste like
from the greener other side

but more and more the open fields are filled
blacktopped the businesslike outskirts
tendrils of the small towns intertwined

till by now the herd animal money crop
people most see is one another
and in all seasons stifle the desire
to crouch by beehive or enclosure
to spot young ones
jumping clean out of their skins
or lean on the top rail at feed time
to catch all the comings and goings on

2

Maybe to see what more there is to living
hold round warm beginnings in their hands
city gardeners on our block kept
chickens that would crow and cluck
expectant brooding triumphant
their rhythms upsetting and waking us
though they would apologize and claim
it was only done to save a buck

for who doesn't know even now
city from country from wilderness
though craving to live on the edge
who doesn't want the end of sprawl
to be able some evening to step out
and walk past the last house
the final streetlight
hear coyote owl meadowlark
look up into deep velvet
at whatall still out there
and not stumble on a construction site

3

Only now for most nuisance value
condos thrown up alongside
a dairy operation whose arabesques
of green slurry plume forty feet in the air
which even without a fair wind carry

don't want nearby all that lowing fragrance
want pristine wide open spaces
somewhere fine print dollars promised
crave empty still cathedral
stands of old growth trees

so we restlessly wander these outskirts
squat upon rich dirt and settle
reach out and surround
take more because someone will anyhow
take more swearing we care more
take more with dreams of importance
that wake to moments of remorse
take more even with a lust
we hoped would in time grow to love

4

And only buckled in place on a long haul
tunneling through the night
through land that still beckons
to all or none of us
certain moments we may run upon
such overwhelming aromas
fields of mint and mown clover
potatoes freshly turned
sun-dried grapes and grains
ripe honeydew and muskmelon
plums and pears

even the damp earth herself
turned in her sleep borne invisible
lifted off vast open spaces
sharing warm breath and release
this instant ours for the blessing
promising all will be fed

Author's Note

Maybe it was the Jesuit training, or the literalism of his early science courses coupled with the heavy recruiting to be a doctor—but there had to be somewhere else to go, something else to do with the handful of change he was dealt. Something that would take the lid off the predictable. Focus things and let him see into life, enough to do something about it. When he found poetry and dug in, in his teens, it was the hardest thing he had yet found, something he knew right away he was bad at, something he knew was impossible, yet wanted badly enough to keep at. Akin to juggling, which he finally acquired at age 56, long after fits of ego and dreams of deftness had passed.

Then there was farming, how it took hold and lasted. Both of his parents were shy country people who had made it in the city, but he could always see past the veneer to what moved them. Country didn't mean simple, it meant rooted and strong. Hard-working, sure, but resourceful. So when they let him play, and then work on farms in the summers it let him know where he was from, who he was and would always be. Why he had those skills and feelings, and what he could do with them.

Not that there's always a clear choice about where to live, what to do. The virus that's eating the planet seems to thrive in great aggregates—cities and suburbs—and that's where much of the fight is. Which brought him to teaching. In the abstract it would be a way to eat while he wrote, but walking into his first classroom was like coming home.

So why is he now setting lead type in his shop, carving wood blocks? And, around the edges, still writing? The answer is, there are many ways of teaching, all necessary. Modeling how it might be done is the oldest, and maybe in the end the most convincing way to spread change and aid growth.